THE FOURTH SISTER

Laura Scott was born in London and now lives in Norwich. Her pamphlet, *What I Saw*, won the Michael Marks Prize in 2014, and in 2015 she won the Geoffrey Dearmer Prize. Her work was featured in *New Poetries VII* in 2018. *So Many Rooms*, her first collection, was *The Guardian*'s Poetry Book of the Month when it came out in August 2019 and in 2020 it won the Seamus Heaney First Collection Prize and the East Anglian Book Award for Poetry.

ALSO
BY
LAURA SCOTT
FROM
CARCANET

So Many Rooms
(2019)

The Fourth Sister

Laura Scott

CARCANET POETRY

First published in Great Britain in 2023 by
Carcanet
Alliance House, 30 Cross Street
Manchester, M2 7AQ
www.carcanet.co.uk

A CIP catalogue record for this book is
available from the British Library.

ISBN 978 1 80017 305 7

Book design by Andrew Latimer
Printed in Great Britain by SRP Ltd, Exeter, Devon

The publisher acknowledges financial
assistance from Arts Council England.

CONTENTS

For Peter

THE FOURTH SISTER

SHORT STORY

There's a story about Chekhov I love and I'm not sure why,
how the night before he left for Sakhalin he was terrified
of being saddled with a bore for a travelling companion
and because the journey was long, really long, three whole months long,
all the way East as far as you could go across Russia's great girth,
he had to do something, but what? Lacking whatever that trait is,
the one that would have allowed him to just say no, he put out a story
instead, or rather urged a friend to unleash it discreetly,
and apparently reluctantly, into the right circles, to let it be known
that although everyone covered up for him, the famous writer
was in fact a drunk and a swindler, a nihilist actually, and, to crown it all
in a final audacious swap, a bore, and if the truth were known,
nobody in their right mind would want to sit next to him. And the story
was so perfect, so balanced between telling and withholding, it worked.

THE SOUNDS

I wanted something else
     Chekhov

You swept the stage, brushed away the old sounds
as if they were dust so your people could come and sit

and talk long into the night, so long and so late they were too tired
to climb the stairs to bed, so they just sat there floundering

out their truths. The sound of the small hours when talk goes big
and baggy and words unclasp themselves and start to

stumble and veer between precision and blur in a single line –
that was the note your people sang. You drew it out,

pulled open the pauses around it, the dips and wells of silence
when the person speaking looks up and sees the others

across the table with their faces in their hands only half-listening
so the words dry on his tongue. But there was something else,

another sound, coiled inside the pauses, like rain falling,
or an old metronome swinging and searching for a beat,

the sound of time's pulse, flowing and slowing.
You heard that and held a shell to our ears so we heard it too,

passing us by like the sisters left on the stage
hearing the band play as the regiment leaves town.

STILL LIFE

If your whole life were a glass and you were to walk into a room
    and find it there, on a window sill, would you love it
without knowing why and find yourself holding it up to the light?
    Would your fingers move up its stem to tilt it left,

then right, before sliding into place around its bowl and half know
    they were encountering the shape of themselves, a space
blown by your own lips? Would it centre you to see yourself
    like that, would the proportions and balance between foot,

stem and bowl strike you as just and fair? Or would you fret
    and feel misrepresented as you ran your eyes over it
and wonder why your life had been turned into glass? Would you?
    I don't think so, I think you'd love it – to see a life

caught like that, a whole life in a single shape. Or would you rather
    the sweep and story of you had been thrown into something else?
A towel perhaps, on a beach in the wind flapping, held in the fingers
    at the ends of hands on outstretched arms. That moment

when it's shaking off its sand and stretching out in front of you,
    the raggy sprawl of a life, your life blown into shape,
the wrong turns and longing of it, the stillness and speed of it held
    there in the air, the arcs of joy and lack of meaning in it,

the boredom and loves of it, the long beautiful beat of it. All that
    unscrolling and flowing into you, and to stay there,
stay here with that, while it's still moving, still breathing
    and not reach out for an end. I think you'd love that.

JULES ET JIM

There's a photo of them dancing on the set,
the dark-haired one so full of intent, as if he were balancing

an egg on the spoon of his face. And the blond one
so different, eyes nearly closed,

profile accidentally haloed by something in the background
so he looks like a saint in a painting.

It's taken in a break, someone put the radio on
and it must have been playing a waltz

because that's the shape the two of them make together –
off-centre, arms out, up and to the side, a lopsided circle

running through their hands. It only does what photos do, freezes them
mid-step, halts their lilting dance across the room

as if one of the gods had clicked his fingers to still a foot,
so it skims the floor forever, heel to toe, hovering.

COVER PHOTO

the horse leaning
        into the gallop

head and tail conjuring
        a perfect diagonal

is the poem
        strung like a cello

spotted with snow
        and the woman

running towards him
        leaning the same way

head and hem
        of her long black coat

a parallel diagonal –
        the woman is what?

TO BE ONE OF THEM

To be a link in that necklace of sisters, to flit between them
and forget sometimes which one I am, the oldest, or the youngest,

or the one in between. To slide into their space and find my way
into the room they spend so much time in, talking and talking,

to feel the pattern in the threadbare rug under the sole of our black
lace-up boots, feel its colours fade and bleed as we pace up and down

flinging out our lines as if we were scattering seeds into the stalls before I flop
down into a chair and sigh, or maybe laugh. To watch the staircase

fold and collapse under the weight of all our talked thoughts piled up
on each other like a litter of puppies scrambling for milk, to talk and talk

to slow life's ruin down by playing it backwards and to love
the sound of it, the note of longing seeping in and out

of me and everyone around me in that room on that stage
and in that theatre and knowing that really, that's all there is.

JOY

So there you were

    laughing

in the middle of all those people.

      I saw you

when I pushed open the windows to let the night in,

      saw how they surrounded you, how they wanted you,

        a bit of you, how they hung upon your words.

So I left the party thrumming behind me

    and came out into the garden – how could I not?

And as I got closer I saw how the air thrilled around you,

      spinning and fizzing

and I wanted to ask you, I so wanted to ask you,

    how long you'd stay

and whether I'd see you again, but I knew

      if I did, as soon as the words left my mouth,

you'd think of leaving. So I drank you in

instead and pointed to the end of the garden,

and there was something about the way you turned,

the line of your neck perhaps

or the angle of your head, told me you'd come with me,

so I asked and you said

yes.

So we peeled away from the others

but then the noise of the party got louder

and they were playing a song

I could tell you loved, and the people rushed

back to the house to dance and you went with them

and who was I to stop you?

EMAIL

he told me what he saw out of his window –

    a bay tree with a glow on it, maybe from a fire

in a neighbour's garden, some bird

        dotting, and then clinging to a lilac bush,

    and a sky that wanted to be blue – and the words sparked

and flickered as if they were a trail to something. So how do I reply?

    My window only shows the sky

        and branches spanning like a hand

into a stretch and anyway there's a square of gauze hanging

    in front of it with its own sewn pattern

        of branches and leaves. But today

with the sky so blue, so blatant and all those branches

    doing their thing – yes. Tell him that.

MURMUR

The millions of starling things
    I'm scared of
        fly up
into my face too thick
    and too fast for me
      to see
    the glossy sheen
of purples and greens
    on their black
      feathers.

THE BORED COWBOY

and what about the blackbird
singing his big strong song
from the heart of the tree?
let's go back to that,
to how loud it was
and how hidden he was
so at first it seemed
the whole tree was singing,
as if every branch and every leaf
had opened its throat,
and how clear and green
the sound was,
stopping me
and drawing me towards it
until my eyes found a path
through the leaves
and I saw him
centre stage,
the garden's own opera singer
flown in that morning,
framed by painted boards
of magnolia leaves,
how everything else
just fell away
as if the cowboy
who slinks in
every day and leans
against the wall
stringing his rope
with trinkets and worries
and spinning it
in a hoop around me

got bored
and dropped it
to the ground
so there was nothing
between me and the sound
and I saw it,
saw the sharp orange beak
open and close –

THESE DAYS

For days and days nothing happens, nothing ever happens unless
you count the birds that come to her. Mostly it's just bits,
sometimes their feet – pronged tendons perched on her
collar bones, twitching like animated twigs when she moves –

sometimes the ruffling sound of the small ones, clotting the air
with their wings when they fly away from her in the garden.
She thinks a whole one got in once – a sleek fat crow
pushed and pecked his way through the webbing of her ribs

with his wing hands and his sharp beak, and settled himself
amongst the branches of her lungs, caw-cawing to her for hours.
And she liked that, the feeling of him there. But he flew off,
she knew he would. Mostly it's their throats that cling to her,

their double-barrelled throats, pulsing and thrilling and beating
like toy-hearts strewn across her, somersaulting, practising,
practising their song in the neck of her woods until it flitted into her
as easily as they did. Those little wrens, nightingales, and thrushes
thrown across the trees, a disbanded choir, forced out of their hedgerows.

Yes, it was their throats that clung to her, cling to me –

FOR THE GIRL UNDER THE TREE

how to get her, to get her
here, for you so you see her and she's not there
on her own under the tree with her spine laid out
across the grass like a newly hatched snake drinking
the sun, half-closing her eyes to look up at the light
bleaching the leaves the same pale green as the caterpillars

how to get you, to get you
there, for her so you're close enough to see the blue
shadows under her eyes and the grass just
touching her ears, close enough to hear the tock of her thought
as she watches the way the colours move

you'd love her, yes love her
but I don't know who you are or who she is so let's leave her
there unseen – the wordless girl under the tree
watching the colours until the ground hurts under her

THE BORING KING

If the past were a tree lying on its side
    and I were to go to it with a saw

in my hands and rest my knee on its trunk
    until I found the stillness

in the blade before I pulled it back and forth
    through the wood, the teeth

might snag on a knot as if it were a piece of bone
    and pictures of me and my sisters

might spark off the teeth. There wouldn't be any
    of you. My bleak father – the King

of an island where the trees don't grow,
    and us the three princesses

who fell asleep the moment you began to speak.
    And as you talked on and on

into the night, our sleep grew sweeter and our hair
    grew longer and thicker around us.

One sunny day we woke to find you gone.

WHAT I SHOULD HAVE SAID AT MY FATHER'S FUNERAL

Let whatever it is that links me to him
   be as weak as the first skin of ice
that grows on the squares of water in the freezer's dark drawer.
   Let me be the dust that slips between
brush and pan, refusing the logic of the family line again and again.
   Let me slide away on the edge of a playing card
across a polished table, bringing the whole structure of triangles
   collapsing to the floor. Let me undo the thread
and unfather myself here in the fray of these words
   so I can walk slowly down the road
where the tall trees grow on either side until I'm out of shot.

LAST WORDS

She said *don't grieve for me too long* and he said *no more jokes now, bye*

    and when you line them up
    side by side
    like that

    they slot together quite well
    as if they were two halves of something
    that once were together –

    a mother and a father maybe?
    Dying

    in different rooms in different beds in different parts of the same city

like the punchline of a joke you don't quite get –

WHAT THE TREES DO

They play with us
they want to be us
they once were us.

A long time ago
one of them
got the heel of a girl

in the fork of its branch,
snagged her like a bird
caught in a bush

flicked her
up into its leaves.
She cried and the birds

scattered so no-one heard
and the tree pushed her
higher and higher

up to where its branches
scratched the sky
and the wind blew her

hair into the leaves,
and the tree thrummed
under her

and the birds' throats
quivered and her ribs
opened and softened

and their tips pushed
through her skin into the bark
and the tree grew around her.

And sometimes you hear her
tapping her fingers
against your window.

THE FIRST SISTER

They can't remember who,
but someone had said she was obtuse.

None of them really knew what it meant
so it didn't brush her with its wings.

It just floated off and left her
untouched and undefined, balancing

on the stair like a note that's slipped off
a stave. They loved her when she did that,

when she stood still on one foot
on the top stair so full of purpose,

but they hated her when she wandered
into one of the low-ceilinged attic rooms

and reached up for the doorframe,
her bent fingers looking

for its ledge so she could swing back
and forth, as if the house had hands

and they were pushing her.

TIME ON THEIR HANDS

a game they played when days were long and time lay down
    and stretched its hours around them as if they

were the sun, a game that fell from the high white sky
    into their laps, a game they knew the rules of

as soon as they played it, when they lay on their backs
    in each other's beds and took turns imagining

a moment that hadn't happened yet, vaulting fearlessly into
    the future of each other's lives, a shifting game

of fine balance where one sister was teller, the other was told,
    where one listened enraptured to the unfolding

tale of herself, while the other iced it like a cake,
    piping details around its corners of what was worn

and what was said and what he looked like, knowing that
    her turn was next, a game that tied them together,

a game that would blow them apart, a game they don't play
    now, a game some other sisters play.

THE FOURTH SISTER

unsung   unrung   undone

      is that me? (oh God) is that me?

Why do those three words toll

      so heavily in my head

did someone slide into my room as I lay

      asleep like the old king

in his orchard and pour them into the dark

      canals of my ears?

All night they've coursed through me

      mingled with my blood

swilled and sluiced their way into my heart

      and now they're me

and I'm them   unsung   unrung   undone

      uneverythinged –

the fourth sister, the one who slips

      the story's collar

IN THE DOORWAY

From your bath you told me of the man in your book,
fleshed him out, so I stopped seeing you

long and lean in the water, your book-holding hand
swaying slightly above it all, and saw him instead, hesitating,

self-conscious for a moment in his powdered wig, adjusting it
in the gilded mirror that hangs in the theatre's long curved hall,

before he knocks on the door
and joins her in her box. And then you went back to your book

and I waited in the doorway, but he'd gone.

THE WRONG MAN

It was in a Chinese restaurant. We were eating seaweed, first time I'd had it, first time I'd been on my own with my godfather and he was talking on and on in a voice that never drew breath, a voice that unscrolled itself like one of those proclamations with handles someone holds in a film and then drops so we see it unrolling down the stairs. He was laying out the case, telling me how he ended up with the wrong man, wrong colour hair, wrong eyes, wrong everything and I'm fourteen maybe fifteen, sitting across the table from him trying to balance ivory chopsticks on the sides of my fingers and stop the napkin sliding off my lap, not knowing what to say because the thing is, I loved this wrong man more than the confiding godfather, especially the wave in his hair, the way he smells expensive and his slightly plummy voice with a half-laugh in it as if there's a joke stuck permanently in the back of his throat. There have been lots more since then of course, but only one who chimed with him. Years later, different restaurant, Italian this time, lots of people around a big table after my father's funeral and I'm talking to an aunt, the youngest and sweetest of his sisters who's telling me of the man she should have married. And as she talks her voice holds him up like a waiter bending back his wrist to carry a plate of oysters, shimmying through the spaces between the tables until I see him, this talked-of man, handsome, holding court in her bedroom, his long legs stretched out, ankles balanced on the edge of her desk before I look up and see my uncle watching us from the other side of the table, his unblinking eyes listening and watering in the slab of his face, a white expanse of cloth between us. My poor uncle.

DARK ARTS

Everyone said she was a spy – the evidence was
overwhelming: fluent in Russian, drove an old Saab,
moved suddenly to Cheltenham, always had the best tickets
for the Bolshoi, drank like a fish but never spilt a drop.

Next morning among coffees and hangovers,
they'd notice that while they'd unravelled, she hadn't
given anything away. My own godmother, a spy.
She didn't pass any secrets to me. She liked

playing games with time, urging me to keep all the glossy
red programmes from the ballet in a drawer, so I could
look back at them in the years to come. I didn't of course,
they're all lost now. Books – that's what she gave me,

heavy hard-backed books I was too young for. One was full of
paintings I didn't want to look at and words I didn't read.
Strange vegetable woodcuts on its cover – a butterbur with leaves
like lungs, a profile of a cabbage, roots alarmingly suspended.

And there were two paintings in there that harrowed me
with a fear I didn't know existed. The first was grainy grey
and of a saint with sad eyes looking up, arms folded behind
his back so his muscular torso was pushed slightly out as if

asking for the arrows to go deeper into him. Three arrows,
but only two trickles of blood, one from the longest in the base
of his neck, cradled at the edge of that little shaded triangle
between tendon and collar bone, the other running almost

in a straight line from the wound in the middle of his bicep.
Those arrows, those terrible arrows, thin enough to carry
a splinter's cruel pain and sear it into the flesh of my fingers
and the matter of my brain as I turned the thick page.

The second painting was busier: a tree and a boat and a man
trying to climb into a hole, and the animals that scared me.
The goose who'd laid its head down on a great silver plate
and curled its neck around the side, offering itself up to be eaten.

And then the pig, the poor pig, trotting around as if
everything was normal, with a v-shaped chunk cut out
of its back and the black-handled knife there, underneath it,
belted through its skin in case you wanted to cut another slice.

I pulled it from the shelf the other day and found myself
playing my godmother's game with time. I opened it and turned
to those pages and there they still were, the pig and the saint
hanging like shot game, their vulnerable flesh teaching me.

PINTURAS NEGRAS

towards the end of his life Goya painted directly onto the walls of his house

In the middle of the gallery as big as the world
there's a room full of his black paintings, fourteen of them
peeled and pulled from the walls after he died
and brought here to be hung in this room. All pig faces
and drowning dogs, ugly fates and giants ripping
off people's heads, screaming and jostling with each other
on every wall, as if the whole world is crying inside this room,
so long and so hard its face is swollen and there's snot
running in great rivers from its nose and the sobs are catching
its breath so its lungs scratch against your ribs – but if you tear
your eyes away and roll them like marbles through
the two arched doorways you'll see half a golden frame circling
a painting of the sea and then, only then, you can breathe.

IN NAPLES

Caravaggio fled to Naples in 1606 after murdering Ranuccio Tommasoni

He liked to look at the women leaning out
over their balconies.

He put one in a picture,
sweating her, painting her

tired still face and her bent thumb
in the hand around the child in her arms dropping mercy,

cool mercy, on the mess of wings and heads, limbs and breasts below
but never a drop for him.

All he had was the dirt and the heat and a price on his head.

In Naples everything
leans, the tall dark buildings

chasing the light out of the sky and the mopeds
weighed down with people snaking through the cars and ambulances.

In Naples I heard a trumpet
thin and high and true, a run of notes sliding

into the evening as the day shook off some of its heat.
And later that night as the dark square lit up with lights in the trees

I saw them pass a baby around like food
her dark hair wet with sweat.

A SONG FOR MY MOTHER

I lost you
like a dog
loses a bone

or a necklace
loses heat and spills
its shape when it's taken off and dropped

link by link
like a snake
uncharmed

left on the bathroom's cold white shelf.
You're a song
I can't play

trapped in the record's black groove
a rib cut short
pushing against my skin.

Long gone, you're long gone but still
I long for you, long to lean into you.
I blink back

the quail bone (you told me once)
stuck in your throat –
and remember

what it felt like
to swallow
its sharp edges.

POOR SEA

The sweet night air is long gone but come to the window anyway
to look at the sea rummaging through its wardrobe of names.

Look how it slides them along the rail with its blue green fingers –
aegean, caspian, black, red, only to pick the one

hanging right at the back – *dead* – that's all it wears these days.
Poor sea, dying and crying, in your heart of hearts you know your salty tears

only make things worse, flooding the shore so we stand knee deep in you
listening, listening, not for Sophocles' sad note, that's long gone too,

but to you, chainstoking, hauling and heaving the great whale weight
of your lungs into the brine. Someone turned the heat up years ago

and that's when it all went wrong, your rhythm blew away
into the clouds and your waves slapped out of time.

Only ghosts flit through you now. Poor sea.

NATASHA AND HER MOTHER

Kneeling there with her thin hair falling around her neck
and her curled hair-pieces unpinned, waiting on the dressing table,

she could be praying but look again and you'll see she's pleading
with death, whispering in his ear, asking him to let her stay a little longer.

And then you'll see the daughter run towards the bed,
laughing as she slips between the sheets. Look how the mother turns

her head as the daughter pulls them apart. Feel the shape
of her words telling the girl to go back to her bed, hear how they turn

at their edges to pull the girl towards her as they pretend to push her away
– a move the two of them have perfected over the years. And so they lie

together in the crook of the night, the daughter turning her mother's hand
in hers, kissing and counting each knuckle as she talks of the men

who will love her. The mother lies in bed listening while
the words slot into place over their heads, and she is young again.

RAIN AND SEA

It turns to me and murmurs in its sleep
something about the rain's face crying into the glass.

The words lie warm between us
but the rain is cold and blown

into tracts that jolt across the window.
It moves into my arms and puts its nose against my neck.

We listen to the wind warming the sea, cooling the rain.
I want to stay in this wooden heart forever

creaking over the grey. I want the waves
to tilt us into sleep.

But already I feel it slipping
out of my arms to go back to the water.

THE MOTHER AND THE SON

They're on a train and he's taller than her now but his hair is still
a bit like hers, especially at the ends where it flicks out around his ears

and she likes that, likes that so much – that they have the same hair –
and she's taking him – no, she's not taking him, they're going together –

to the crossroads where she'll leave him. All she has to do is follow
the tracks cut deep into the ground like scars left by those who've been here

before. Sometimes, she sees faces pressing against the window, or looking up
at their carriage as it flies past. She thinks they were there, watching her

when she first brought him home, murmuring to each other as they moved in
closer to catch the smell of him as he lay in her arms. And now, the faces,

they're telling her to leave him – *no* – they mouth at her through the window,
don't watch him, you mustn't do that, turn away so you don't see him step down

and walk away into the sea of people. But the thing is he's like a present, the best
    present
she has ever had, and they know that, and still they tell her to walk away,

so she does.

43

IN PANDORA'S BOX

Suppose I'd had another, and called her Hope,
because she was, you only had to look at her
to see that. And suppose she hadn't slid off my knee

and walked away like the others –
what would that have been like? To have Hope
here sitting at the table, swinging her legs,

colouring in pictures of waterfalls I'd draw for her
with all the blues and greens she could find.
I'd feed her cakes made from oranges and almonds

and in between mouthfuls, she'd look up
and if I looked sad, she'd fly to me like one of the
imploring sparrows from Mr McGregor's garden

and unsnag me with her cakey fingers. And when
she was older we'd talk about what it was like to be left
in that box, how her name almost drained away

when the curious woman slammed down the lid
once she saw what she'd let out. And I'd listen to her
in astonishment – how she always knew she'd get out.

RESTAURANT WINDOW

She told me she'd seen two birds, a brother and a sister, or maybe a mother
and a baby, she wasn't sure but they were flying

across the sky. She went to look again. This time she saw trees,
lavender trees she said. She said they were dancing in the air. And as she told me

I saw her mind moving in her eyes like a bird
                                        on the other side of the glass.

THE LINE

I

That day we swam

in a juddery line across the smooth Greek sea

from one side of the horse-shoe bay to the other

further than either of us had ever swum before

right out to the rocks she wanted to jump off. And every time I turned

back   there she was   at my heels   the girl I made –

her head above the water – the girl who'd swum and spun deep

inside me before I even caught a thought of her.

That's what I want you to see – us in the water.

I want to float that   into your head, to hold it

there   still for a moment

before I show you me   turning back   to look at her the very moment

the line breaks so you see her

treading water and readying herself to find her own true line.

2

but there wasn't a line and if there was, it didn't break.
It tightened and knotted, tugged until it hurt. And I didn't let go.

I hung on like her hair, slicked back by the sea, hung to her
skull so you could see the dents in her temples glistening

in the sun. I imagined her falling and hitting the rocks before
she disappeared under the waves. But still we swam to them

and when we got there we let our arms float and dropped
from horizontal to vertical and scissored the water with our legs.

I felt her purpose lap away into the sway of the sea. And her body
clouded into the water like ink until it was my body falling

and hitting the rocks before it split in two as if I'd fallen
into some terrible myth where one half of me shielded the cub

of her from the rock's sharp edges while the other turned the sea
red with blood, rinsing and washing my fear into her.

3

What am I trying to do anyway?   to get the truth, to crow it

    like a caged bird   you fool, you fool

for love is fierce and craggy like the rocks

    and you already know the last line, you always have,

                    let go

THE PHOTOGRAPHER'S DAUGHTERS

So that's what you do –

    return, repeatedly

to your girls, your porous girls

    you've poured so much into as if they

were your true still life, but these girls

    are anything but still, they billow

and smoke though the house,

    making new shapes of themselves,

growing longer and smoother everyday

    like their brown blonde hair –

and you watch them and they let you

    and forget you as they raise their arms

up into a party's warm air, or hold a bottle

    horizontally to their lips with one hand

and span the other across their flat bellies to still

all the life in there waiting to get out.

You've got them covered and uncovered as they

lean against a front door, with the strap

of their silver shoes slung over a finger. Your still

lens taking you just up to their edge.

SAD TALES BEFIT MY WOE

                    said the Duchess
in our daughter's play, and before I knew what that meant,

the words swam into me and lodged themselves in my ribs
and lay there

skulking and waiting like a flat fish under my lungs quivering
and frilling its edges, stirring clouds of death into the muddy water

and now all I know is woe. It has taken my eyes and leeched their blue,
puffed up their lids so all I see is you

gone, or you split into bits and scattered through the house, you
as a photo behind glass, your wit strung out across an email.

You not with me. That's what I see.

I swam to you years ago, around you, under you, next to you,
and I swim for you now

and when the flat fish first beckons you down
I'll follow you and circle you

and push you back up with the silver arch of my back

back up towards the light

where we can see the rain pepper the surface
and feel its warmth on our oily flesh.

There's always another move
and this is the sideways one where they slide

into her dreams but they're wrong – wrong size, or there's only one
when there should be two.

But there they are moving like fish around her calves in the middle of a road
cars streaming past on either side.

The cars are big and fast and the children are drifting outwards
(but it's beautiful because they have no fear).

So she bends down to the boy first and tries to lift him, to sit him
on whatever it is that's floated into place to be sat on

but he is taller and heavier than she is
long and lean with hands as long as thigh bones;

as for the girl, she is slippery, so slippery and the look in her eyes –
she'd never let herself be picked up.

They're just there
in the middle of it all, cars streaming past on either side.

WHEN DEATH GOT BORED IN THE HOSPITAL

Everything fell into place like a sheet
thrown across a bed, spreading as it falls.

You were there on your own
and we talked until our voices turned into splints

in a parasol, pushing the blue rice paper out
into its pattern of birds spreading their wings

above our heads, shading us from the heat
of what was happening to you. And death

got bored of watching us so he left the room
and found somebody else to stand next to,

but when the parasol started to collapse
he must have heard the sound of its bamboo ring

sliding down the stem, because he came back
and watched as we struggled to keep it open,

smiling to himself because he knew
there was nothing we could do to stop the birds

tucking their wings back into their bodies,
locking their pattern away into the blue creases.

THE THERAPIST

for Ursula

I didn't like your name
at first, I couldn't hear
the bear prowling

around in it,
but as the weeks
spun into months

something changed.
And I did. Maybe it was
saying it more – the soft sound

of the first syllable,
the way those three letters
seemed to lean

into each other. Or maybe
I just got used to it,
the same way I got used to

coming to your room
with the marble eggs
on a low table between us

and you sitting across from me
with your well cut voice
and your pleated skirt.

Or maybe it was the hint
of a growl in your laugh
as you unknotted me

or the way your ringed fingers
danced with your words,
clever as bear claws,

carefully passing the apple
of me between them
and it didn't bruise.

WHY ARE YOU SILENT?

a poem made from the letters between Olga Knipper and Anton Chekhov

Another day and no letter from you
Life is so dreary without them
For the love of God write, I'm waiting, I'm waiting

> I would like to write to you
> but I can't

Write me a beautiful letter
Write what you feel, write what you want,
whatever your pen dictates

> I can't think of anything new or
> interesting
> Most of the time it is boring
> and boredom is useless and absurd

I live a stupid absurd life
oh how tedious it is to live
even more tedious to know the tedium
is your own

> everything is as it was, I expect nothing
> it has been raining quite stupidly for two days

the dampness here, the grey
lowering skies

> damp centipedes are climbing the walls
> frogs and baby crocodiles are playing in the garden

I want to see you awfully
I so wish you were here
I would chat to you about joy and sorrow.
I would set out a game of patience
with nice, torn cards

                                        your hand
                        I kiss your hand, hard, hard, hard!
            don't forget me otherwise I shall drown

remember me
I remember you
and the way we discussed Uncle Vanya and I was dying
with laughter inside

                        I took some powder – heroin –
                            and I feel pleasantly calm

Do you love me? Do you believe me?
Are you lonely without me? Do you eat well at dinner?
Do you quarrel with your mother?
Are you kind to Masha? Try and answer
all my questions from now on. Write more
about yourself, tell me everything

                I have nothing to offer – oh yes, one thing:
                            I caught two mice today

I just wanted to tell you I have such a strong desire
to live a happy life. You're not laughing at me?
You do understand? Tell me, do we really
understand even a fraction of life?

        write the essentials so there won't be two stamps on the envelope

I write appallingly like a schoolgirl
I'm ashamed of my letters, terribly ashamed!
There's nothing of me in them, nothing of my real self

                                        where are you?
                    a century has passed without a letter from you
                                        what does it mean?
                    I really love it when you talk about things
            Your sweet, glorious letters give me unusual pleasure

Come quickly I want to see you

                                                    I'm swimming

CHEEKBONES

She found herself thinking of his more and more,
it was a kind of game she played where she had to

find the right word for them, the one with the frisson
of a direct hit and 'elegant' was the closest she'd got.

Can you even have elegant cheekbones? She only ever
talked to him at parties and the parties seemed to be

drying up. He wasn't even at the last one. She'd scanned
the room for him, but he wasn't there. Maybe that's why

she was thinking about the cheekbones and how they
took his face out of time so she could imagine it younger

and older in the same swoop of thought. She liked his talk,
the way he made silhouettes for her of the people there.

That was all really – but here she was still plucking over
the strings of his face, trying to find his note.

YOUR EYES

If someone were to ask what colour
    they are I wouldn't say

anything, anything at all. I'd sit there
    silent as a spy before I turned

to look out of the window.
    Maybe I'd light a cigarette

and by the time the smoke escaped
    from the side of my mouth

they'd forget they ever asked.
    But if someone were to ask

what they're like, I'd tell them
    everything. I'd sing your eyes

like a canary. I'd tell them
    they're hooded like a bird of prey's,

how they never blinked,
    how they waited and waited

for me to break cover
    and how nearly I did.

I'd tell how they pulled me taut
    for you, caught by you,

and how even now the slip
        of a thought of them makes me

want you, takes me back
        through a door to you.

HARE

I don't know who saw you first, I like to think it was me
and maybe it was, but there you suddenly, undeniably were,

the same colour as the earth coming towards us as we stood
in our quartet of black on the edge of that field. A relic

from the old world slipped through into this one, ancient
as tapestry, you coursed the trench between the stubbled crops

and then you stopped and tuned your black-tipped ears to the sky.
When you were still I knew what you were, but when you leapt

into the air, taking off from nothing, shape-shifting in front of us,
I didn't. Handsome hare, for days now you've been running

through my head. I'd slip for you and fall into blind devotion,
opening myself up like a sail to all the sighs of belief that still cling

to your brown coat, if you can do what they say and box
the thought of my love, cold and gone, out of my field of vision.

MUSE

I played you

      in the fibres of my head

  as if you were a note and I was a piano

someone had opened up   pushed back all my black

  my strings and hammers left exposed –

LA SCALETTA

I left it
in the hotel
hanging
from a hook
on the back
of a bathroom
door, a long
sheath of ivory
silk
running
all the way
from spaghetti straps
to scalloped hem
just skimming
the floor,
a web of black
lace blown
around its neckline.
I came back
and found it
laid out
in a flourish
on the bed
arranged
so it darted in
at the waist
and the skirt
flared
out
across the cover,
transformed

into what
it had always
wanted
to be.

RAIN

Draw the curtain and you'll see it
   swarm around the street light,

and then you'll see it everywhere –
   in the grass bowing its head,

semi-circling back to the earth,
   on the dog slicking her stripes

dark on her ribs, or even the blue bowl
   of noodles, as if this rain

is making them plump again.

THINKING OF TONY HOAGLAND

   crying in his poem about Leonard Cohen,
coolly circling his tears, thinking what they mean
and where they come from as they run down

his face and he looks out of the window
at it nearly sleeting and the cars and the headlights.
And now of the silver birch in our garden,

how it's watched us so long two eyes have appeared
on its trunk, one on top of the other,
how under the lower lid of each, the wood is stained

and dark and runs in vertical lines down the bark
so it looks like they're crying too. But why do I always
think like that? It's an abstract pattern of renewal

made by rings in the surface marking where a branch
once was and anyway, why would watching us
make it weep? It's just a tree in a garden

we've spent so much time in, so much, as if we were rich
as kings in hours and days spent talking and talking
about all the big things and all the small things

while the tree grows taller and broader, and we
pick up its twigs, rake up its leaves,
circling and circling the silver birch.

THESE LINES

All these lines to remember, all these lines you'll forget –
the lines of birds forming and breaking,

breaking and forming, breathing an imperfect V
across the sky. And the lines that crease

our palms, blown across our hands, heart lines, life lines,
folding and deepening, starring and intersecting,

lines the palmist longs to see. And the lines that fissure
and suture the skull, fusing plates of bone

together to shield the yolk of brain. Rilke dreamt
of playing them, of running a needle

across their groove so he could hear those wavering lines
scratch out their truth. All those lines

meandering, drawn by the same thing, all those lines
to remember and lines to forget.

ACKNOWLEDGEMENTS

Thanks to the editors of the following publications in which some of these poems have appeared: *And Other Poems, Bath Magg, PN Review, The Rialto, Poetry Ireland Review* and *The London Magazine.*